Native Americans

The Ohlone

Barbara A. Gray-Kanatiiosh

ABDO Publishing Company

visit us at
www.abdopublishing.com

Published by ABDO Publishing Company, 8000 West 78th Street, Edina, Minnesota 55439. Copyright © 2002 Abdo Consulting Group, Inc. International copyrights reserved in all countries. No part of this book may be reproduced in any form without written permission from the publisher.

Printed in the United States of America, North Mankato, Minnesota.
012002 122011

Illustrations: David Kanietakeron Fadden
Interior Photos: Corbis
Editors: Bob Italia, Tamara L. Britton, Kate A. Furlong, Kristin Van Cleaf
Art Direction & Maps: Neil Klinepier

Library of Congress Cataloging-in-Publication Data

Gray-Kanatiiosh, Barbara A., 1963-
  The Ohlone / Barbara A. Gray-Kanatiiosh
    p. cm. -- (Native Americans)
  Includes index.
  Summary: Presents the history, culture, daily life and religion of central California's Ohlone people, who were nearly destroyed when Europeans entered their land, and who are fighting today for recognition by the Bureau of Indian Affairs.
  ISBN 1-57765-603-2
  1. Ohlone Indians--History--Juvenile literature. 2. Ohlone Indians--Social life and customs--Juvenile literature. [1. Ohlone Indians. 2. Indians of North America--California.] I. Title. II. Native Americans (Edina, Minn.)

E99.O32 G73 2002
979. 4'0049741--dc21

2001045893

About the Author: Barbara A. Gray-Kanatiiosh, JD

Barbara Gray-Kanatiiosh, JD, is an Akwesasne Mohawk. She has a Juris Doctorate from Arizona State University, where she was one of the first recipients of ASU's special certificate in Indian Law. She is currently pursuing a Ph.D. in Justice Studies at ASU and is focusing on Native American issues. Barbara works hard to educate children about Native Americans through her writing and Web site where children may ask questions and receive a written response about the Haudenosaunee culture. The Web site is: www.peace4turtleisland.org

Illustrator: David Kanietakeron Fadden

David Kanietakeron Fadden is a member of the Akwesasne Mohawk Wolf Clan. His work has appeared in publications such as *Akwesasne Notes, Indian Time*, and the *Northeast Indian Quarterly*. Examples of his work have also appeared in various publications of the Six Nations Indian Museum in Onchiota, NY. His work has also appeared in "How The West Was Lost: Always The Enemy," produced by Gannett Production, which appeared on the Discovery Channel. David's work has been exhibited in Albany, NY; the Lake Placid Center for the Arts; Centre Strathearn in Montreal, Quebec; North Country Community College in Saranac Lake, NY; Paul Smith's College in Paul Smiths, NY; and at the Unison Arts & Learning Center in New Paltz, NY.

Contents

Where They Lived 4

Society 6

Food 8

Homes 10

Clothing 12

Crafts 14

Family 16

Children 18

Myths 20

War 22

Contact with Europeans 24

Pomponio 26

The Ohlone Today 28

Glossary 30

Web Sites 31

Index 32

Where They Lived

    The Ohlone (ah-LONE-ee) lived along the Pacific coast in central California. The Ohlone are sometimes called Costanoans. This name comes from Spanish explorers who called the Ohlone *Costeños,* which means "coast dwellers."

    The Ohlone spoke a Costanoan language. There are eight Costanoan languages: Karkin, Ramaytush, Chochenyo, Tamyen, Awaswas, Chalon, Mutsun, and Rumsen. These languages come from the Utian language family of the Penutian language stock.

    The Ohlone homelands covered a large area. They were home to many different groups of Ohlone. The homelands were located as far north as the southern shores of San Francisco Bay. From there, Ohlone homelands stretched south from Monterey Bay to Point Sur.

    The Ohlone homelands had oak forests and grasslands. Water was plentiful. The land had many freshwater streams and rivers. Beautiful beaches and marshes covered the land along the ocean and bays.

The coastline near Point Sur

The Ohlone Homelands

Society

    The Ohlone lived in villages. Each group had its own territory and villages. The villages could be as small as 50 people, or as large as 300 people. An average village contained about 200 people.

    The Ohlone also lived in camps for part of the year. Temporary camps were used when the whole community was needed to gather seasonal foods, such as acorns.

    Each Ohlone village had a council of **elders** and a chief. They protected and advised the people. The title of chief belonged to a family. It was usually passed on from father to son. If a chief did not have a son, his sister or daughter could serve as chief.

    The chief had an assistant. The assistant gathered items for ceremonies. He also invited other villages and nearby tribes to join in ceremonies or trade.

    War leaders kept the peace. They also protected the people from hostile tribes. Medicine people were spiritual leaders. They healed people and performed ceremonies to ensure good hunting and fishing trips, and bountiful harvests.

An Ohlone village

Food

The Ohlone hunted, fished, and gathered foods. They hunted deer, elk, antelope, rabbit, and ground squirrel. They also hunted birds such as doves, quail, and geese. Along the coast, the Ohlone hunted for sea lions and beached whales. The ocean also provided seafood such as clams, mussels, and octopuses.

The Ohlone hunted with **rabbit clubs**, bows and arrows, traps, and nets. They used shell and bone hooks, woven traps, and nets to catch fish such as steelhead, salmon, and lamprey. The meat was dried in the sun, roasted, or cooked in an earthen oven.

Acorns were an important food to the Ohlone. The whole community camped near oak **stands** to gather acorns. They used long poles to knock down the acorns. The Ohlone crushed the acorns into meal. They used the meal to make mush and bread.

The Ohlone also gathered seeds from dock and chia plants. The Ohlone hit these plants with seed-beater baskets. This knocked the seeds into a collecting basket. The seeds were roasted in a basket with hot coals, and then eaten.

The Ohlone also ate fresh berries and roots. They gathered strawberries, gooseberries, and clovers. They dug up roots such as amoles, cattails, and wild carrots. The Ohlone also ate honey, yellow jacket **larvae**, and roasted grasshoppers.

An Ohlone woman making acorn mush

Homes

    The Ohlone lived in different types of homes. Many lived in dome-shaped homes. They made the frame from willow poles. They covered the frame with thatch made from **tule** (TOO-lee), grass, or alfalfa. The Ohlone used strips of willow to attach the thatch to the frame.

    Some Ohlone lived in cone-shaped houses. They were made from large slabs of redwood bark tied onto a willow frame. The doors were covered with mats or animal skins.

    Inside, each home had a fire pit in the center. The Ohlone used the fire to heat their home and cook food. They made beds from tule and furs. Blankets woven from rabbit fur kept the Ohlone warm at night.

    Another type of building the Ohlone constructed was a sweat house. Often the Ohlone built a sweat house into the bank of a stream. Men often took a sweat bath every day. They believed it purified the body.

In the center of the village, there was a gathering place. It was surrounded by a brush fence that was about four and one-half feet (2 m) high. In some villages, these dome-shaped buildings were large enough to hold all the villagers!

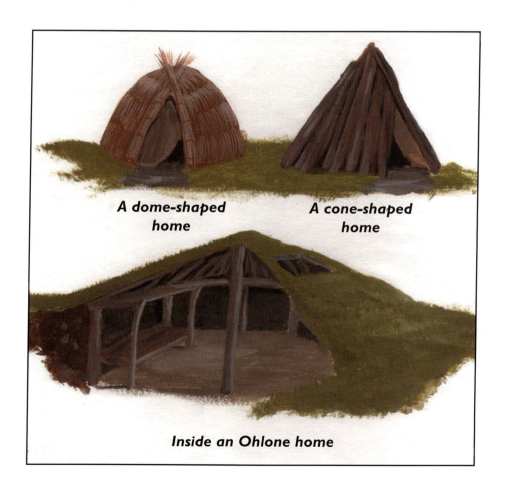

A dome-shaped home

A cone-shaped home

Inside an Ohlone home

Clothing

    Ohlone men and boys often went naked. When not naked, they wore **breechcloths** or kilts. They were made from buckskin or rabbit skin. Men also wore headbands with feathers standing up on the front.

    Women wore aprons. The front aprons were made of braided **tule**. The back aprons were made from buckskin or woven sea otter skins. Sometimes women wore net skirts with feather fringes over their aprons. These skirts were woven from Indian hemp or milkweed fibers.

    During the colder months, the Ohlone wore fur robes and blankets. They made the blankets from sea otter skin, rabbit fur, or duck feathers.

    Men and women **tattooed** their faces, arms, and upper bodies. They used a sharp piece of flint or **obsidian** and charcoal to make the tattoo. The designs were made with dots and straight lines.

Men had long hair, which they often braided. Sometimes the men tied their hair on top of their heads in a bun. Women had long or shoulder-length hair. Sometimes they had bangs.

Men and women wore necklaces and ear jewelry made from bones or shells. They also painted their bodies. They used clay to make white paint, and a mineral called hematite to make red paint.

An Ohlone family in traditional dress

Crafts

    The Ohlone made **tule** boats. They used stone axes to harvest tule from wetlands. Then they tied the tule together in a long bundle. They tied all the bundles together to form the boat. Tule boats could be 10 feet (3 m) long and hold up to six people. The Ohlone used the tule boats for fishing and duck hunting.

    The Ohlone also made musical instruments. They used single, hollow, bird bones to make whistles. They crafted flutes from pieces of wood. Split sticks of laurel served as rattles.

    The Ohlone made twined and coiled baskets. They used the baskets for storage, cooking, and gathering. Seed-beater baskets were used to harvest seeds. These baskets were shaped like spoons. A woman would insert the basket into the plant containing seeds. Then she would shake the basket, and the seeds would fall into it.

An Ohlone man playing a flute

Family

If a man wanted to marry a woman, his family gave gifts to the woman's family. If her family accepted the gifts, the marriage was approved. The woman moved into the house of her husband's father. Sometimes a man had more than one wife. A man's second wife was usually his first wife's sister.

The whole family lived in the same home. Often a family included grandparents, aunts, uncles, and cousins. They lived in the same home or nearby in the village.

Each person in the family had a role. Men hunted and fished. Women gathered wild berries, greens, and roots. Women also prepared the food for eating.

Men, women, and children all gathered acorns. Women spread the acorns on the ground to dry. Then they pounded them into flour. Women poured water over the acorn flour to remove any bitterness. When the bitterness was gone, the acorn flour could be cooked and eaten, or stored for later use.

An Ohlone man uses a pole to knock acorns from a tree while an Ohlone woman gathers the acorns in a basket.

Children

Children were raised by their extended family. They learned the language, history, songs, dances, and ceremonial ways of their people. They learned how to hunt, fish, and gather by helping their families.

Women carried their babies in cradle baskets. The cradle was made from willow or **tule** woven to form a U-shaped holder. Mothers used handwoven straps to carry their babies on their backs.

Young boys learned how to make basketry traps from willow. Fish traps were often long and had a round, wide opening that narrowed at one end. Fish swam into the wide end and soon became trapped in the narrow end.

The boys also learned how to make duck **decoys** from willow. They shaped the willow so it looked like a duck. When placed on a pond, the decoy attracted real ducks.

Young girls learned how to cook food in baskets. Baskets were woven so tightly they could hold water without leaking. Girls learned to place hot rocks in baskets filled with water. The hot rocks heated the water. Then they mixed acorn meal with the hot water in the basket to make acorn mush.

Children also had time to play games, such as shinny. The object of the game was for one team to move a puck to the other team's goal. They played shinny with long curved sticks that looked like hockey sticks.

An Ohlone boy with a duck decoy

19

Myths

    After Coyote created the land and people, he taught people to survive. Coyote said, "See those puddles on the beach?" The people nodded their heads, yes. Coyote said, "You will look for those puddles after the tide goes out. In them you will find good things to eat like mussels, clams, and stranded fish." He said the people will get salt and seaweed from the water.

    Then Coyote handed the people a bow and arrows. He told the people how to make them, and showed them what to hunt. He said, "See those large animals? You will eat the deer, elk, and antelope."

    He handed the people a long pole. Coyote said, "See those trees over there? They are oak trees. The acorns that grow on them will be your most important food." He told the people how the acorns had to be prepared to get the bitterness out. He showed them the kinds of berries, greens, seeds, and roots that people could eat.

Coyote taught the people how to give offerings and thanks for the food. He said, "Do not offend the lives you take. Offer them tobacco and prayers. If you do, they will return next year."

Coyote gives an Ohlone man a bow and arrows

War

The Ohlone rarely went to war. Their **economy** was based on trade. So they needed to keep good trade relations with nearby tribes. The Ohlone traded items such as salt, kelp, abalone, seaweed, and mussels with inland tribes. For these goods, the Yokut people traded piñon nuts, and the Miwok people traded clam shells and clam disk beads.

If a neighboring tribe **trespassed** on Ohlone lands, the Ohlone would fight. Oak **stands** and seed fields had to be defended. Protecting their food source was a matter of life and death for the Ohlone.

The Ohlone fought wars with bows and arrows. A war leader led his people on surprise attacks. Sometimes a war leader arranged a meeting with the tribe that trespassed. If peace could not be kept, then war was arranged.

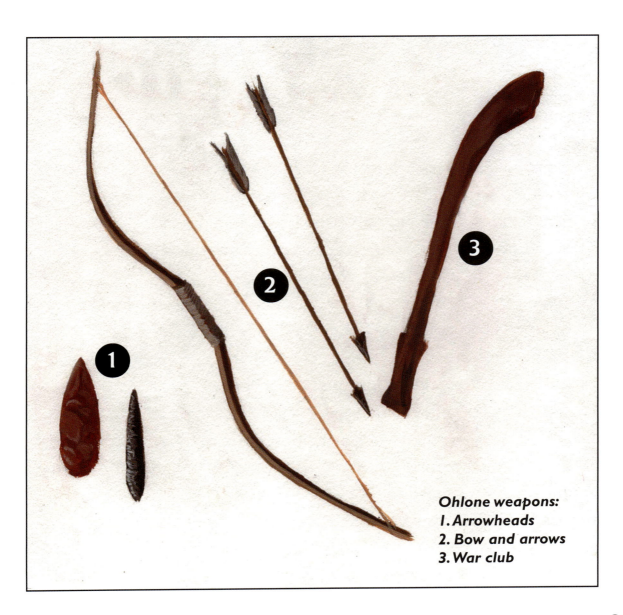

Ohlone weapons:
1. Arrowheads
2. Bow and arrows
3. War club

Contact with Europeans

Europeans began exploring California's coast in the 1500s. In 1542, Juan Rodríguez Cabrillo explored the coast for Spain. Englishman Sir Francis Drake sailed along California's coast in 1579. Then in 1602, Sebastián Vizcaíno explored Monterey Bay as a possible site for a Spanish colony.

After Vizcaíno's journey, Europeans did little with the California coast for nearly 100 years. Then in the 1700s, Spanish priests began building **missions** on the California coast. Seven of these missions were on Ohlone homelands.

Priests at the missions hoped to convert the Ohlone to Christianity. Those who became Christians were forced to give up their traditional ceremonies and religions. They had to move onto the mission grounds and work.

After the Europeans came, many Ohlone lost their lives. In 1770, there were about 10,000 Ohlone. By 1832, less then 2,000 Ohlone remained. Diseases brought by the Europeans killed many Ohlone.

This was a very sad time for the Ohlone people. They lost much of their traditional ways and also their lands to the Europeans.

A Spanish priest with an Ohlone man

Pomponio

Pomponio was an Ohlone chief. He was a brave man who struggled to save his tribe's way of life.

In the 1820s, Pomponio led his people in resistance against the **missions**. He did not like the way the missions forced the men and women to work for them. He did not like that his people were forbidden to do their ceremonies and social activities.

The Ohlone were not free to leave the missions. The missions became prisons. When Ohlone people escaped, soldiers hunted them down. Some Ohlone were punished for leaving, and others were killed.

In 1824, Pomponio died at the hands of soldiers in a place called Novato. He died trying to protect his traditional way of life.

Chief Pomponio

The Ohlone Today

Today, there are about 550 Ohlone. They are fighting many legal battles. They want to regain their lands and be recognized as a tribe.

The Ohlone lost their recognition as a tribe in 1927. That year, the **superintendent** of the Bureau of Indian Affairs in Sacramento ended federal recognition of the Ohlone, as well as several other California tribes. For this reason, the Ohlone do not have any federally recognized **reservations** or **rancherias**.

In the 1980s and 1990s, many Ohlone tribes **petitioned** for federal recognition. But the process is long. Many tribes have been waiting more than 10 years to learn if they will be federally recognized. Today, these tribes continue to wait for a decision from the government.

Federal recognition is important to the Ohlone. It would allow the Ohlone and their children to be eligible for grants, scholarships, and other funding. The funding would help the Ohlone to strengthen and restore their traditional ways.

A rocky cove near Big Sur, located on Ohlone traditional homelands

The coastline just south of Monterey Bay, also part of Ohlone traditional homelands

Glossary

breechcloth - a piece of hide or cloth, usually worn by men, that was wrapped between the legs and tied with a belt around the waist.

decoy - a fake bird used to lure real birds to within shooting distance of hunters.

economy - the way a tribe used its goods and natural resources.

elder - a person having authority because of age or experience.

larvae - insects in the early stage of development.

mission - a center or headquarters for religious work.

obsidian - a hard, glassy rock that is usually black. This rock is formed when lava cools.

petition - to make a formal request to a person of authority.

rabbit club - a weapon thrown at a running rabbit's legs that snares the legs and trips the rabbit, keeping it from running away so the hunter can catch it.

rancheria - a tract of land reserved for Native American use. It is usually a smaller portion of the tribe's original homelands.

reservation - a piece of land set aside by the government for Native Americans to live on.

stand - a group of trees.

superintendent - a person who directs the work of a business or institution.

tattoo - to permanently mark the skin with figures or designs.

trespass - to unlawfully enter another person's property.

tule - a reed that grows in wetlands.

Web Sites

Muwekma Ohlone
http://www.muwekma.org/
The official site of the Muwekma Ohlone has up-to-date news on the tribe and a detailed history section.

Ohlone/Costanoan Esselen Nation
http://www.esselennation.com/
Learn about the tribe's name, its traditional homelands, and its history.

These sites are subject to change. Go to your favorite search engine and type in Ohlone for more sites.

Index

B

boats 14
Bureau of Indian Affairs 28

C

Cabrillo, Juan Rodríguez 24
ceremonies 6, 7, 18, 24, 26
children 12, 16, 18, 19, 28
Christianity 24
clothing 12
cradle baskets 18
crafts 14

D

dances 18
Drake, Sir Francis 24

E

English 24, 25

F

family 16, 18
federal recognition 28
fishing 7, 8, 14, 16, 18, 20
food 6, 8, 9, 10, 16, 18, 19, 20, 21, 22

G

games 19
gathering 6, 8, 9, 14, 16, 18

H

hair 13
harvest 7
homelands 4, 24, 25
homes 10, 11, 16
hunting 7, 8, 14, 16, 18, 20

J

jewelry 13

L

language 4, 18
leaders 6, 22, 26

M

marriage 16
missions 24, 26
music 14, 18
myth 20, 21

P

Pomponio (Chief) 26

R

rancherias 28
religion 21, 24, 26
reservations 28

S

Spanish 4, 24, 25, 26

T

tattoos 12

U

U.S. government 28

V

villages 6, 11, 16
Vizcaíno, Sebastián 24

W

war 6, 22
weapons 8, 20, 22